Waiting for a Jamie Oliver:
beyond bog-standard literacy

cover illustration by
Quentin Blake

ISBN 0704998483

National Centre for Language and Literacy
The University of Reading
Bulmershe Court
Reading RG6 1HY
www.ncll.org.uk

Designed and produced by Text Matters
www.textmatters.com

Contents

Chris Powling

Bog-standard literacy

Two years ago, a handful of children's authors – backed by almost a hundred of their colleagues – published a collection of essays called *Meetings with the Minister* (NCLL, 2003). This was intended as a howl of protest at what we saw as the devastating narrowness of the National Literacy Strategy. Also, it was an account of our attempts to persuade the Minister and his advisers at the DfEE that immediate action was needed to remedy the damage the strategy was doing to children's reading and writing for pleasure.

Well, we can't claim the booklet was ignored. The publicity it attracted gave a new lease of life to our campaign.

Charles Clarke, then Secretary of State for Education, had been both polite and attentive. His officials continued to be encouraging. Professor David Hopkins, for instance, who chaired a number of the meetings, declared more than once that 'there was little of substance between us'. A range of possible counter-measures were discussed. One or two have already been put in hand – such as the contribution of professional children's authors to the new Teachers' TV Channel and the input of children's librarians (where these were available) to teacher-training courses. There was even some public acknowledgement of the kind of issues that concerned us – notably by the Chief Inspector of Schools, David Bell, in a speech to mark World Book Day earlier this year:

> Reading has always been seen as a source of considerable pleasure for many. This is important, but has perhaps been forgotten by some schools in their pursuit of higher test results that will improve their position in the league tables. You will find no pleasure in books if you cannot read, but it is equally possible to be able to read and derive little pleasure...

Not that every school allows this to happen. According to the report *Reading for purpose and pleasure* (Ofsted, 2004) at least some were addressing the problem:

> ... [here] pupils had opportunities that extended well beyond the typical literacy hour to practise and to improve their reading skills.

> Reading had a high profile in the curriculum with time given to it in addition to literacy lessons, such as using the library and the reading of a class novel... *One school with particularly high standards in reading actively promoted a love of literature throughout the school* [our italics].
>
> SOURCE: www.ofsted.gov.uk/publications/index.cfm?fuseaction=pubs.summary&id=3805

One school?

Out of a sample of forty-five?

And there's the rub. The truth is that paragraphs 92 and 93, from which the above extract is taken, stick out from the report as a whole like a couple of petunias in an onion patch. The main thrust of the argument remains plonkingly purposeful, in the familiar heads-down mode, as if the word 'pleasure' in the title were the merest afterthought. Perhaps we were naïve to expect anything else. After all, the report was launched last December with a three-and-a-half page press release in which the word 'book' is never mentioned. So much for our powers of persuasion. For all we know, other similar titles are already in preparation – 'SATS and enjoyment', perhaps. Or maybe 'The pleasure of league tables'.

Yet our cause remains compelling. It's hardly a revelation that there are two competing ways to conceptualise literacy:

- as a skill-based activity which demands discipline, practice and repetition
- as a means of making the world meaningful... with motivation and appropriate materials at a premium.

As professional writers, we recognise the validity and the necessity of both approaches (though not necessarily in that order). If only the National Literacy Strategy did the same. Its relentless prioritising of the first, by way of drilling and testing and 'texts', has so undermined the second that bog-standard literacy is now not merely the norm but presented as some kind of success story. In reality, its modest achievements are bought at an extraordinary price. According to figures gathered by The Educational Publishers Association, the state system currently spends somewhere between three and six times as much on testing as it does on books.

Yes, *really.*

Some of the essays which follow were written especially for this booklet. Others are re-printed here with the permission of the author and the original publisher. All of them are frankly sceptical of a pedagogy which teachers tell us prompts many children to punch the air with delight whenever the Literacy Hour is cancelled.

Philip Pullman

Common sense has much to learn from moonshine

First published in *The Guardian* on 22 January 2005, Philip Pullman's article was written in response to a piece of educational research which in itself should give Literacy Strategists pause for thought.

The report published this week by the University of York on their research into the teaching of grammar will hardly surprise anyone who has thought about the subject. The question being examined was whether instruction in grammar had any effect on pupils' writing. It included the largest systematic review yet carried out of research on this topic; and the conclusion the authors came to was that there was no evidence at all that the teaching of grammar had any beneficial effect on the quality of writing done by pupils.

Needless to say, this goes against common sense. That particular quality of mind, the exclusive property of those on the political right, enables its possessors to know without the trouble of thinking that of course teaching children about syntax and the parts of speech will result in better writing from them, as well as making them politer, more patriotic, and less likely to become pregnant.

For once, however, common sense seems to have been routed by the facts. If we want children to write well, giving them formal instruction in grammar turns out not to be any use; getting them actually writing seems to help a great deal more. Teaching techniques that do work well, the study discovered, are those that include combining short sentences into longer ones, and embedding elements into simple sentences to make them more complex: in other words, using the language to say something.

A word often flourished in this context by the common sense brigade is 'basics'. It's always seemed curious to me that commentators and journalists, people who write every day, and who presumably know something about the actual practice of putting words on paper, should make such an elementary error as to think that spelling and punctuation and other such surface elements of language are 'the basics'. These, and deeper features of language such as grammar, are things you can correct at proof stage, at the very last minute, and we all do that very thing, every day. But how can something you can alter or correct at that late point possibly be basic? What's truly basic is something that has to be in place much earlier on: an attitude to the language, to work, to the world itself.

And there are many possible attitudes to take up. There are some that are confident and generous and fruitful, and others that are marked by fear and suspicion and hostility. We instil these attitudes in children by the way we talk to them, or the fact that we don't, and by means of the activities we give them to do, and the environments we create to surround them, and the games and TV programmes and stories we provide them with. The most valuable attitude we can help children adopt – the one that, among other things, helps them to write and read with most fluency and effectiveness and enjoyment – is one I can best characterise by the word playful.

It begins with nursery rhymes and nonsense poems, with clapping games and finger play and simple songs and picture books. It goes on to consist of fooling about with the stuff the world is made of: with sounds, and with shapes and colours, and with clay and paper and wood and metal, and with language. Fooling about, playing with it, pushing it this way and that, turning it sideways, painting it different colours, looking at it from the back, putting one thing on top of another, asking silly questions, mixing things up, making absurd comparisons, discovering unexpected similarities, making pretty patterns, and all the time saying 'Supposing… I wonder… What if…'

The confidence to do this, the happy and open curiosity about the world that results from it, can only develop in an atmosphere free from the drilling and testing and examining and correcting and measuring and ranking in tables that characterises so much of the government's approach, the 'common sense' attitude to education.

And the crazy thing is that the common sense brigade think that they're the practical ones, and that approaches like the one I'm advocating here are sentimental moonshine. They could hardly be more wrong. It's when we do this foolish, time-consuming, romantic, Quixotic, childlike thing called play that we are most practical, most useful, and most firmly grounded in reality, because the world itself is the most unlikely of places, and it works in the oddest of ways, and we won't make any sense of it by doing what everybody else has done before us. It's when we fool about with the stuff the world is made of that we make the most valuable discoveries, we create the most lasting beauty, we discover the most profound truths. The youngest children can do it, and the greatest artists, the greatest scientists do it all the time. Everything else is proofreading.

Take the National Curriculum. The authors of the York study remind us that it lays down that children from 5–7 'should be taught to consider a) how word choice and order are crucial to meaning, b) the nature and use of nouns, verbs and pronouns,' and so on; that children from 7–11 'should be taught word classes and the grammatical functions of words, including nouns, adjectives, adverbs, pronouns, prepositions, conjunctions, articles,' as well as 'the grammar of complex sentences, including clauses, phrases and connectives…' Think of the age of those children, and weep. It simply doesn't work.

What does work, the York study maintains, is writing in a meaningful context: writing as a practical hands-on craft activity. One of the implications of this is that teachers themselves have to be confident about writing – about play: about delight. Too many of them are not, because they haven't had to be; and the result is the dismal misery of the 'creative writing' drills tested in the SATs, where children are instructed to plan, draft, edit, revise, rewrite, always in the same order, always in the same proportions, always in the same way. If teachers knew something about the joy of fooling about with words, their pupils would write with much greater fluency and effectiveness. Teachers and pupils alike would see that the only reason for writing is to produce something true and beautiful; that they were on the same side, with the teacher as mentor, as editor, not as instructor and measurer, critic and judge.

And they'd see when they looked at a piece of work together that there were some passages that were so good already that they didn't need rewriting, that there were some parts that needed clarifying, others that needed to be cut down, others that would be more effective in a different order, and so on. They'd see the point of the proofreading, at last; and they'd be ready, because they were interested, to know about the subordinate clauses and the conjunctions and the rest. The study of grammar is intensely fascinating: but only when we're ready for it.

True education flowers at the point when delight falls in love with responsibility. If you love something, you want to look after it. Common sense has much to learn from moonshine.

Jamila Gavin

Creativity... and risk

Playfulness, then, is a crucial aspect of Creativity. So is the taking of risks. Neither is very amenable to the following of rules and regulations – the preferred mode of those who insist all learning should be *tidy*. Jamila Gavin explains.

Tony Blair said recently, that we can't expect to live in a no-risk society. Yet it feels increasingly as if we are all Gullivers, pinned down by a myriad of edicts, laws, targets, assessments and strategies, dominating every aspect of our lives. In practice, we are denied the right to take risks, to be wrong, to fail and, as Becket famously said, "try again and fail better," in case this risks the government not achieving its own targets.

What if there had been a law saying don't sit under apple trees in case one drops on your head?

The adult artist is often desperately trying to claw back those first wondrous experiences of childhood and discovery; that wild imaginative world – often secretive, extraordinary beyond the adult's wildest imagination. What we should be seeking is to till the child's rich imaginings, not destroy them with the production values and killer pesticides of an overly-prescriptive curriculum.

This is not to say that there shouldn't be any targets. The child may be born a noble savage, but it has to face the reality of a highly structured and complex world – so of course it must achieve literacy and numeracy at the very least, but further, and vitally, must learn to think constructively, critically and philosophically. Children must learn the craft of learning, and have the tools of acquiring knowledge and articulation at their disposal.

And yet...

Study after study after study has shown that if every child – not just the so-called gifted child, but *every* child – had, of right, access to the things which inspire and stir the imagination and creativity, then this would actually cause them to perform better all round. Philip Pullman calls it play; playfulness; things such as music, drama, dance, art, poetry, reading and writing. Play is the life force of creativity – it's the life force of a healthy society and feeds like a healthy diet through every other aspect of their lives – not just the arts – but the sciences too. They say we have a dearth of children going into science. Could this be exactly because there is a failure to stir their imagination? To be scientific is to be creative, imaginative and playful too. This is why I passionately believe the arts must be part of every child's healthy diet, and must continue to be the soul of every society. They inspire us to learn with a purpose, gain confidence, articulacy, and have a dynamic and inter-active regard for the world around them. True education is having faith in the human condition; that people are born curious and thirsting for knowledge; that when they see something which can nourish and benefit them, they will reach for it. But we have devised a system that amounts to force feeding – and far too many of our children are sick.

This is where I come back to risk. It surely starts in teacher education. If the teachers are trained well, and given the confidence to go out and contribute their individual talents and skills, the government could risk being less prescriptive, have a more flexible curriculum, and allow for more imaginative ways to keep our children – and teachers – engaged with the education system.

Children first hear the words 'creative' and 'imaginative' from teachers, asking them to write a poem or a story – as though it's the prerogative of the English lesson. English and its handmaidens, creativity and imagination, should be in attendance at every lesson. Many children believe books are written to order – if only you learn the right formula. They don't grasp that for the 90 percent perspiration, you have to have that 10 percent inspiration – at the very least. Take them outside, up a mountain, to a theatre or a concert, then ask them to be creative. Show them how life, nature, and raw human experience has inspired the most marvelous works and inventions, so that they too can be inspired.

You can't be creative to order. No one can. Not unless you can move freely through that wilderness of curiosity, discovery and resourcefulness – the way children can put two chairs together and create a train or a space ship; the way a blanket over a table becomes a house, or an underground world of other beings; the way a wander through an orchard, sitting under an apple tree can lead to the discovery of gravity. What are our equivalents? No longer can even a primary school teacher respond to a sunny day and say, "Let's go out and see how many trees we can identify, or frog spawn we can spy!" I visited a city academy specializing in science, who therefore saw no necessity for providing their children with the experience of putting on a school play, or playing in an orchestra.

So what am I asking for – realistically – not as an impossible pipe-dream?

In our highly diverse society with literally thousands of stimuli whirling around us, I'm asking that we are more selective with what we give our children in school. We should recognize that, for a vast majority, it may be the only opportunity to give them contact with the finest achievements of many civilizations. I think a fear of 'elitism' has meant that generations of children aren't hearing the finest music, reading the finest literature, or being given access to the best of human achievement. I want, on the one hand, to allow children to show *us* what it is to be creative and imaginative, but on the other hand for us to give them shining examples of the best we know: to learn the best grammar and vocabulary because we have given them the best books to read; have encouraged them to learn by seeing and doing; that possibly less is more; give them a less but more selective best, but with more time to absorb what they're given. If there is a literacy hour on the timetable, let there also be a silent, reading hour; an hour to listen to good music, an hour simply to think – and hours to take on a whole book rather than extracts.

I believe that if we can restore to our children time, trust, and emotional safety – so that they can go outside over there, where the wild things are, they will return inspired, creative and confident; people ready and willing to take on the world.

Why don't we take the risk?

Michael Rosen

Children's reading

On 8 March 2005, Michael Rosen was installed as a Visiting Professor at the University of Middlesex. What follows are a few brief extracts from his inaugural lecture, delivered aloud and offered here unaltered.

Let's begin with education. It's in schools where most people not only learn *to* read, they learn *how* to read. For many people, outside of the regularly book-reading minority, this is the one place where they will learn what reading *feels* like; and what reading is *for.* It's the critical moment when either the reading bug might bite or give up trying. Now, the world of children's books has always existed in a symbiotic relationship with education, with schools looking to children's literature for books to read; and children's literature looking to schools to buy their books for its libraries and classrooms, and for schools to create active readers who come back over and over again to read more books.

But what's going on with books in schools? Many of us here have been witness to the fact that the way books are read in schools has, over the last four or five years, changed. We are full of anecdotal evidence of, say, years 5 and 6 classrooms where whole books are *not being read*; where books are being chopped up into fragments which are then turned into worksheets; and these fragments are then used as examples for exercises on spotting verbs and similes.

We can offer eyewitness accounts of how the word 'literature' has been abolished. It is, as you know, now called, 'literacy'. So this has turned the act of reading into a performance to be assessed: how well is he reading? Is she reading *accurately*? Is she reading *fluently*? How can we *test* this reading performance? How can we create a set of classroom activities around reading that will be testable so that we can show that a child is reading at this or that level?

For those of us who write children's books, let alone for the hundreds of thousands of people who enjoy the business of reading books with the children they know, we're pretty sure that this is *not* why we got involved. The reasons why we write books for children are complex and diverse but amongst them you can find a notion like: *wanting to say things that matter to young people*. And when I say, 'matter' that can take in such ideas as wanting to intrigue, entertain, educate, amuse, excite, stir up and challenge our audience. I don't know many writers of books for children who would say, "I write children's books so that a class of year 5 children can count the adjectives on page 43 of my latest novel".

But let's leave the anecdotal evidence to one side, and even my wistful complaints about what's happening to our precious book in schools. In fact, looking at the people in this room makes me think we should set up an open and independent commission to look into exactly how books are being read in schools at the moment. And before that, to set the field, we could invite people who have thought long and hard about why we read and enjoy literature, to offer some thoughts. And then we could match these thoughts with what is actually going on. I have a picture of taking let's say AS Byatt, Derek Walcott – I don't know – John Carey, Germaine Greer into a set of primary schools to see a classroom preparing for a SAT reading paper and asking our visitors if what's going on matches up with what they think literature is for. Come to think of it, it might make an interesting documentary...

It's one of the curious ironies of our time, that children's literature has been discovered at precisely the moment that large sections of the public arena are intent on avoiding a discussion about children's books that treats them just as we might talk about books for adults.

It's hard not to get conspiratorial about it. Or should I say, structural? It can't be an indifference about literature in general because books are getting as good a whack from the media as they've ever got. It can't be to do with the lack of interest in what, as adults, we think we're doing with our kids. So where's the problem? To tell the truth, it's a problem this culture has with children themselves.

The difficulty surrounding books for children is that they are unashamedly on the side of children. They also suggest that children should be taken seriously... that how children think, feel and behave is something that matters. This is implied both in what the stories seem to be about, but also the very manner in which they are presented, the very fact that they are presented at all. We say: here is something that you may well enjoy, you are someone worth entertaining, have a laugh, get scared, be amazed, be bewildered.

What children do, think and feel is well below the radar of the prevailing ideas of the powerful. It doesn't feature as part of public discourse. A possible reason for this is that though children rate as consumers (or their parents on their behalf) they don't rate as producers. Rather like Old Age Pensioners. They don't make anything, so they matter less for what they are, only for what they will become; they're not a state of being, they're a state of being on the way to somewhere else, called adulthood. Again, an ironic state of affairs considering the massive rise in therapies that place our adult lives in the grip of our childhoods. It's as if we're saying, children are boring, but my childhood is fascinating... let me tell you about it...

So, this thing we're in, books for children, has to struggle with this structural indifference. A structural indifference that always mouths that books for children are worth reading, but rarely puts its money where that mouth is.

I think you only know if books are worth reading if you have a chance to find out what you think of books – and it helps a lot if you have a chance to find out if anyone else wants to hear what you've got to say. I suggest that the starting point for this is for a curriculum that puts the reading of whole books back on the agenda. It also suggests that the best way to ask children questions about books is either to *ask none, or to ask questions that the questioner doesn't know the answers to.* Questions like: does this book remind you of anything you've met in real life? Or remind you of anything you've *read* elsewhere? When you compare the book with these things you know from your life and from your reading, what similarities and differences do you spot? Is there anything about this book that puzzles you? Is there anybody in the room who thinks they can help with this problem? Is there anything you like or dislike about this book? Why's that then? Is there anything we would ask any of the characters in this book? Is there anywhere we can go to find out answers to any question we have about this book?

For most of us in this room, as I said at the outset, the question is hardly worth asking – are books for children worth reading? We know it. For many children though, this is not self-apparent. We have to *prove* it to them.

Bernard Ashley

Children's writing and SATS at ks2

Writing well is difficult enough under optimum conditions. Under exam-conditions it's almost impossible – especially if your handwriting is also being assessed. One of our favourite moments while talking to Charles Clarke came when Bernard Ashley produced a photocopied page from the notoriously illegible manuscript of *Bleak House*. "Enough to get Dickens a level four?" he asked. Here, abbreviated from a paper written for a later meeting, Bernard draws attention to other conflicts of interest.

It came to me in the early summer of 2003 that I was confusing these year 6 children. Invited into the school as a visiting author who would talk about his books, where his ideas come from, and how a story develops, I was into the section of the talk where I describe my working methods when I suddenly realised that these poor children would be sitting their ks2 SATs test in writing the following week. I was doing them no good, because I was contradicting what they would have been taught about writing for the test. And Chris Powling, Philip Pullman and Jamila Gavin would all have told them something different again – because writers have to find their own ways of putting their words on paper. Rather than teach a set of rules about writing, children should be enthused and encouraged to experiment in every aspect of the art. Writing by formula is no more art than is painting by numbers, although it does have the advantage of being fairly straightforward to assess.

Unless children already want to write as they might want to skip the pavement instead of walking it, to dance instead of watching from the side of the hall, to sing with joy instead of voting for someone else to be a Pop Idol – then what they write will be so many words on paper that someone else will need to be paid to read. If they write as a chore, it's read as a chore: and reading someone's writing should be part of a celebration, not part of a calibration.

The other day my youngest grandson asked me what a metaphor was. I was pleased with the question, until he told me he'd asked it because his teacher said that if they put some metaphors into their SATs writing test they'd get extra marks. What a waste of six years' primary education! I ask children to imagine being the first person out of the building after a snowfall, when their footprints will be the first mark made on the open space; or to imagine being the first into the empty swimming pool, the water calm and inviting, where will they make the first splash – this end, that end, by jump or dive? Then I tell them that that is how I look at a blank sheet of paper. Not to 'face' it as an adversary, but to know that I can inscribe it for my pleasure – perverse and difficult as that pleasure may be.

We should ask ourselves why we write imaginatively at all. Isn't it for pleasure, as a personal resource – a working out, a demon chase, a dance before the hunt – an exploration of a great plot idea, or the birth of an intriguing character? If these are the sorts of reasons for giving time to writing in school, should we even attempt to assess four years of such eclectic writing in a 45 minute examination? Dare teachers say to their classes, "Go in and write your souls out, and fail dismally, if that's the way it goes today"? Of course not, they want SATs success for their children and their school, because otherwise they slide down the league table.

In the schools I visit almost weekly, I come across very few who don't work in Years 5 and 6 towards the SATs. What a waste of two years when those children could have been developing into real writers in a writing confident society.

So how can writing best be assessed – because it's no part of my argument that children's progress in school shouldn't be assessed (nor that writers should stop going into schools). We get mathematical answers right or wrong; we get scientific formulae right or wrong; we get spellings right or wrong; we can read certain words or we can't. Some of these things can be measured. But how can we measure the imaginative spirit – this child against that child against a norm – as it is evidenced in one piece of writing? We can't. And where does it take us by doing so, anyway? Who does it help, except the politicians in some spurious appeal to middle England?

I think we must recognise that the sort of 'real' writing being considered is not one of the 3Rs at all – it's one of the 3As, with Art and Music the other two; and we accept that there are secretarial and *referential* sorts of writing that *can* be assessed by test, but that *poetic* writing (James Britton's terms) cannot; in which case we free up teachers from other things and assess children's writing by portfolio; a portfolio used for assessment – but which is really a portfolio of a child's early life in writing – to carry with them if they wish, as the word implies.

In the mid-70s Sir Alec Clegg addressed an educational conference at Goldsmiths' College, his subject 'The shadow and substance of education'. His description of reactions to the rote learning of his father's and his grandfather's day sadly bears more than passing resemblance to the bored and uninspired attitudes of many modern children in our schools, who can't wait for the doors to open; whose poor behavioural tendencies are not suppressed by the cane anymore, but by threats of exclusion from Ruth Kelly. Excitement, experiment, creativity at the heart of our education system, with rigour in its proper place – when we see that we need it – would transform the atmosphere in so many boring, test-success driven primary schools functioning as young grammar schools which deprive children of the excitement, experiment and experience of the 'primary' years – the three Es.

As his conclusion, Sir Alec said this:

> … on this business of the balance of goads and spurs, we might consider what was written in the testimonial that Michelangelo took to the Pope, who was to employ him on the building of the Dome of St Peter's and on the painting of the Sistine Chapel. This is what it said: "The bearer of these presents is Michelangelo, the sculptor. His nature is such that he has to be drawn out by kindness and encouragement, but if he be treated well, and love be shown to him, he will accomplish things that will make the whole world wonder."

What drives us with SATs is not excitement, experiment and experience but fear – and when was fear ever creative?

A quartet of laureates

Among the most distinguished members of the children's book world are our four Children's Laureates. Below, each of them remarks on an aspect of literacy which causes them concern… except Quentin Blake. Instead, he drew the cover illustrations (thereby reminding us that children's books offer an education in images as well as words). Implicit in every piece is a recognition that the surest route to successful writing is successful reading.

Michael Morpurgo

Bring back the book

The government's markedly laissez-faire attitude to book provision in schools contrasts sharply with its hands-on approach to other aspects of the curriculum. It's now possible, by combining SATs with School League Tables, to rank-order every child in the country as a reader/writer. What *isn't* possible, apparently, is a system which guarantees each child's book entitlement or even the availability of a local and properly-funded Schools Library Service.

It's easy for people to see the benefits of good food and exercise. But the benefits of books are far less obvious. Governments like things they can measure and for which they can set targets to show they are doing their job properly, so education has become ever so more focused on delivering an extremely narrow set of results. Along the way, books have become marginalised – mere educational tools – and everyone from teachers to pupils has lost some of the magic of reading.

Of course, we have to ensure that everyone reaches the basic standards of reading and writing, but how are you going to achieve that without first giving children a sense of fascination and wonderment for books? That means putting books and storytelling at the heart of school life.

It's almost certainly true that those schools that have invited me to visit over the past two years are the ones that place the most value on books, but even in these schools there's rarely an embedded culture of a love of books. And almost invariably where there is something approaching such a culture it's entirely down to the enthusiasm of a single teacher.

In roughly half the schools I visit, the level of book provision is extremely poor: the library is little more than a few books in a corridor and the children have one textbook to share between three. This subconsciously places a low value on books in the minds of children and inhibits their ability to learn.

Where textbooks have a narrow remit – a sole purpose of getting a child through a set curriculum – they are unlikely to be that educationally challenging. Teachers and children will pick up on this and switch off. However, the boredom is less a function of the book than the system itself.

We need an education system that prepares children for a challenging world in which they become active participants in a democracy, not one that teaches them to do a limited number of measurable tasks unthinkingly. To achieve this, we need to put books back at the heart of school life.

Michael Morpurgo, in conversation with John Crace, *Education Guardian* 12 April 2005

Jacqueline Wilson

Libraries and librarians

I'm very pleased and proud to be the most borrowed author in our public libraries (even though it makes me sound rather shabby and well-thumbed!). Like nearly all the authors I know, libraries have played an immensely important part in my life. As a child I had one single shelf of books, mostly tattered Puffins and those leatherette two-and-sixpenny classics you used to buy at Woolworths. I loved reading and reread my favourite books many times, but of course I wanted *new* books to keep me going. We were strapped for cash when I was a child. I had a book for my birthday, and maybe a paperback as a summer holiday treat, but that was it. I liked to read several books a week, and I was definitely a book-a-day girl during the holidays. I therefore haunted the public library. It was just one rather dark and dreary room way back in the fifties, with one of those cartoon stereotype librarians forever raising a finger and saying Sh! – but to me that room was fairyland and the librarian a true fairy godmother who waved her blue biro and let me borrow as many books as I liked.

It's so good to know that children must still be using the libraries. Even in the age of multiple television stations and the computer children *do* still enjoy reading books. Librarians don't lurk in dark silent rooms nowadays. They do their level best to make their libraries lively vibrant colourful places, as child-friendly as a carnival. With limited resources they organise fantastic holiday reading events, they go into schools and do story-telling sessions, they organise many author visits, they valiantly dress up as Peter Rabbit and Postman Pat at summer fairs.

They want to reach the children who *don't* read, the homes where there are no books at all. I've never met a children's librarian yet who isn't committed and enthusiastic and desperate to spread the word that reading is *fun*. It seems criminal that so many specialist children's libraries and branches of the Schools Library Services have had to close down. We need many *more*, please! Let's celebrate these tireless and wonderful professional people who do so much to get children hooked on books.

Anne Fine

Read, read more, read everything

Read. Read more. Read everything. It's the advice offered by all good writers and it's the advice most often ignored in schools.

Strange, that. After all, reading is a treat. You're indulging yourself and, if you're reading aloud bringing pleasure to others. Books furnish minds, and everyone – *everyone* – comes to their own style through absorbing or refracting the styles of others whilst painlessly picking up tricks of the trade.

More and more of our children now come through school with none of this experience behind them. It's as if a host of clockmaker's apprentices had been set to pick apart the tiny workings on the bench in front of them without anyone thinking to teach them how to tell the time. Some children claim to leave primary school never having read a whole book and we authors get stacks of letters along the lines of, "Our teacher read us a little bit of your Bill's New Frock." (What on earth happened to class sets?) Or, "We looked at the start and the end of your story."

Children can't *guess* how the magic works. They have to feel it: the gradual opening up of the tension of the story; the arching middle when all the characters and themes have been woven in place; the breathtaking hover before the satisfactory wind-up. Oh, you could tell a child how a high-wire act can be exciting. Easier, surely, to take them to the circus and let them gasp.

Instead, we set even the youngest onto futile tasks like planning, drafting and redrafting, ploughing through wedges of text only to pick out the similes. Meanwhile, the standard of creative writing gets worse and worse. Last week a despairing school librarian told me, "None of our children read". I asked the head if I could invite an author to get them excited. Guess what she said "No, I don't think so, George. The Year 8s are already doing a book this term and we don't want to confuse them".

Thirty years ago, this woman would have been carried out of any school by men in white coats. We must get back to a state of affairs where teachers read widely enough to encourage their pupils, not only by example, but at an individual level. "Here, Larry. You're into gore. You'd like this novel. Jan, you're always scrapping with your sister. Have you tried this book?"

Only a reader can become a writer. That's why we give the advice we do: Read. Read more. Read everything. It's the only way.

Quentin Blake

Sometimes a picture is worth a thousand words...

That's why we shifted Quentin Blake's contribution to our front – and back – covers. Check his maths as well. This also tells a story.

Alison Prince

Magic books

One government minister quite unembarrassed at contradicting a Philip Pullman article is David Miliband. Below, in a letter to *The Guardian* in October 2004, Alison Prince replies to the Minister's reply – and sums up for many of us the sheer absurdity of asking children to behave like book-experts before they've become book-enthusiasts.

David Miliband talks of 'the false choice between enjoyment and excellence'. This skewing of Philip Pullman's argument betrays a failure to see what a child's enjoyment of a book really means. It is a head of emotional steam that supplies immense energy and an exhilarating sense of expanding horizons. Once fired by this, a child can easily become interested in the nuts and bolts of how this magic has been achieved, but without it, the paraphernalia of questions and analysis is a dead duck. Children need the skills of writing, yes – in fact, they deserve them – but the carrier-wave of fascinated enjoyment must come first. At present, the two processes are back to front.

Chris Powling

Book-standard literacy

In two respects, we're told, the Literacy Hour has transformed the primary classroom for the better. Firstly, we now have an approach to reading and writing that's both consistent and co-ordinated. Secondly, it rids us at a stroke of the sort of pick-and-mix, fingers-crossed amateurism which was allegedly so widespread before the ring-binder revolution.

Or so the theory goes. In practice, one glance at this particular ring-binder confirms the truth of Karl Popper's wry observation that the problem with revolutions is their tendency to be held in thrall by what they're reacting against. In this instance, so determined was the DfEE to leave nothing to chance, or to individual teachers, it devised a regimen fit for a zombie. How else can you describe a programme that's so congested it's riddled with more bullet-points than the St Valentine's Day Massacre, so prescriptive its launch-movie actually featured the ringing of a bell to signal changes in classroom activity, and so charmless in tone and vocabulary that even where fun is hinted at you don't believe a word of it.

What a wasted opportunity!

At our first meeting with him, Charles Clarke reminded us that he was "not in the business of lowering standards." Almost in unison, we replied: "Neither are we!" On the contrary, what we were after was the *establishing* of standards in those aspects of literacy which mass-testing passes by – standards which it seems are taken seriously by only one school in forty-five. How can children learn to think for themselves, we wanted to know, if their teachers are forbidden to do so?

We're still waiting for an answer. Altering course is no simple manoeuvre for a ship of state the size of Education – especially when so many careers and reputations are committed to full-steam-ahead. Will the QCA's rumoured new initiative 'English 21' seek to improve matters? And even if it does, will its recommendations be acceptable to Ruth Kelly our latest Secretary of State for Education?

Altogether, Mike Rosen's suggestion about some sort of TV documentary begins to look more and more alluring. Thanks to Jamie Oliver, it certainly worked for school dinners. How hard can it be, after all, to demonstrate the superior nourishment of a novel over the turkey twizzler of a 'text'? For books, proper books – in all their richness, completeness and variety – lie at the heart of real achievement in both reading *and* writing. Admittedly, they can also be awkward and unpredictable. Perhaps we shouldn't be too surprised that the National Literacy Strategy chose to cut them down to size in the interests of classroom convenience… and thereby left a gaping hole in its own credibility as a raiser of standards. It's time we lifted these from 'bog' to 'book'. Edith Sitwell once famously described poetry as "language-on-tiptoe." What are books if not literacy-on-tiptoe?

Books bring another bonus, too. Any teacher who's run a successful book week, organised an author visit, or just read her class a full-length story, will have experienced this at first hand. They give us the best possible opportunity to see kids punch the air with delight when an *extra* hour of literacy is announced.

The contributors

Chris Powling is the author of more than 60 books, mainly for younger readers, including *The phantom carwash*, *The multi-million pound mascot* and *Blade*. He's a regular broadcaster and was editor of the magazine *Books for keeps* from 1989 to 1996 when it won the Eleanor Farjeon Award for distinguished service to children's literature.

Philip Pullman won his first awards, and great popularity, with books like *The firework maker's daughter* and *Clockwork*. His career went stratospheric, however, with the trilogy *Northern lights*, *The subtle knife* and *The amber spyglass*. It also killed off, hopefully forever, the notion that children's books are doomed to represent a lesser form of literature than those written for adults.

Jamila Gavin followed her widely acclaimed *Surya* trilogy (*The wheel of Surya*, *The eye of the horse* and *The track of wind*) by winning the Whitbread Prize with *Corma Boy*. Her novel *Grandpa Chatterji* was televised on Channel 4.

Michael Rosen has been instrumental in taking poetry out of the ghetto and into the hearts and minds of children with collections of his own poetry, anthologies and performances. As a journalist and broadcaster, he is an important ambassador for children's books, arguing that they should be taken just as seriously as every other branch of literature.

Bernard Ashley won the 'Other' Award in 1974 with his first novel, *The trouble with Donovan Croft*. Since then, his sharp, compelling narratives of inner-city life, often reflecting his own experiences as a head teacher, have been both popular and critically acclaimed. Several, such as *Running scared* and *Dodgem*, Bernard has successfully adapted for television.

Michael Morpurgo has written over forty books including *Why the whales came* which was made into a major feature film, and *My friend Walter*, filmed by Thames Television. *Kensuke's Kingdom* has been a hugely successful novel, and has won a range of prestigious awards. In 1978 he and his wife Clare started the charity farms for City Children, which they still run, and for which they were each awarded an MBE in 1999.

Jacqueline Wilson has written over 80 books but her real success began with *The story of Tracy Beaker* published in 1991 when she was first paired with the illustrator Nick Sharratt. Since that time *The story of Tracy Beaker* has sold over a million copies and has become a major drama for the BBC. Sales of Jacqueline's books now exceed 20 million copies.

Anne Fine is a distinguished novelist for both adults and children. She has won all the major awards for children's fiction, several twice over. Her many books for all ages are widely read in schools, from *Bill's new frock* at primary level through to *Flour babies* and *The tulip touch* for older readers.

Quentin Blake has illustrated over 250 books by many writers; notably John Yeoman, Russell Hoban, Joan Aiken, Michael Rosen and most famously, Roald Dahl. He is also well known for his own picture books such as *Clown* and *Zagazoo.* He was appointed as the first Children's Laureate in 1999. Other awards include the *Chevalier des Arts et des Lettres* and the IBBY Hans Andersen Award for Illustration.

Alison Prince wrote *How's business* with primary school pupils as co-authors, and still works constantly with children, last year creating an opera with three schools in Leeds, and currently helping 140 Bradford children with a multi-arts work on the young Brontës. A poet and biographer, she has written over 50 children's books, many of them prize-winners.